COLOR

New & Easy Decorating Library

BETTER HOMES AND GARDENS® BOOKS
Des Moines, Iowa

New & Easy Decorating Library
Better Homes and Gardens® Books An imprint of Meredith® Books
Published for Creative World Enterprises LP, West Chester, Pennsylvania
www.1CreativeWorld.com

COLOR Volume 1
Project Editors: Denise L. Caringer, Linda Hallam
Art Director: Jerry J. Rank
Copy Chief: Catherine Hamrick
Copy and Production Editor: Terri Fredrickson
Contributing Copy Editor: Margaret Smith
Contributing Proofreaders: Kathy Eastman, Colleen Johnson, Gretchen Kauffman
Electronic Production Coordinator: Paula Forest
Editorial and Design Assistants: Kaye Chabot, Mary Lee Gavin, Karen Schirm
Production Director: Douglas M. Johnston
Production Managers: Pam Kvitne, Marjorie J. Schenkelberg

Meredith® Books
Editor in Chief: James D. Blume
Design Director: Matt Strelecki
Managing Editor: Gregory H. Kayko

Director, Sales & Marketing, Retail: Michael A. Peterson
Director, Sales & Marketing, Special Markets: Rita McMullen
Director, Sales & Marketing, Home & Garden Center Channel: Ray Wolf
Director, Operations: George A. Susral

Vice President, General Manager: Jamie L. Martin

***Better Homes and Gardens*® Magazine**
Editor in Chief: Jean LemMon
Executive Interior Design Editor: Sandra S. Soria

Meredith Publishing Group
President, Publishing Group: Christopher M. Little
Vice President, Consumer Marketing & Development: Hal Oringer

Meredith Corporation
Chairman and Chief Executive Officer: William T. Kerr

Chairman of the Executive Committee: E. T. Meredith III

Creative World Enterprises LP
Publisher: Richard J. Petrone
Design Consultants to Creative World Enterprises: Coastline Studios, Orlando, Florida

All of us at Better Homes and Gardens® Books are dedicated to providing you with information and ideas to enhance your home. We welcome your comments and suggestions. Write to us at: Better Homes and Gardens Books, Shelter Editorial Department, 1716 Locust St., Des Moines, IA 50309-3023.

If you would like to purchase any of our books, check wherever quality books are sold. Visit our website at bhg.com or bhgbooks.com.

CONTENTS

New & Easy Decorating With Color

Color is one of the constants in our lives. We learn, work, think, and daydream in color. From the time we wake until we go to sleep, we live among the changing colors of nature—from the pale roses of sunrise to the vibrant oranges and purples of sunset to the inky blue-black of night. From earliest childhood, we all have natural color preferences—favorite hues that warm our lives and soothe our souls. These colors lift our moods or remind us of pleasant memories. A sunny yellow recalls family times in the kitchen; a cool green, our grandmother's

Getting STARTED

favorite vase. Drawing on all those influences, we can create our own environments based on the colors and objects that make us happy. When you choose your personal palette, no doubt you have some givens—a favorite painting, an upholstered chair, a collection of plates—to guide you. In the home, *opposite,* new countertops repeat the hues of treasured pottery, and a small, but influential, primitive stool inspired the bold new coat of barn-red paint on the back door. **Start by thinking of the colors you love,** then use this book, which focuses on classic color categories and palettes, to find compatible companions for them.

Use the color wheel as a tool to create your personal palette. In a glance, this "rainbow in the round" demonstrates the relationships between colors. For a quick visual test of your own preferences, pick a color you like from the wheel, then look around the wheel to see what color you would use with it. Let's say you love blue. Would you accent it with, say, hot orange or yellow—or cool green or purple? Your answer will give you a clue to how much contrast your eye prefers.

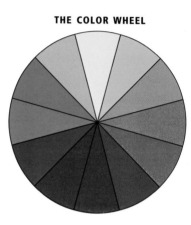

THE COLOR WHEEL

For a quick and compatible palette, choose a triadic scheme that blends any three colors equidistant on the wheel. The primary colors—blue, yellow, and red—form a a classic triadic palette that works equally well with country, traditional, or modern styles. The secondary colors—green, orange, and purple—also work beautifully together. Remember that although we've shown pure hues here, all colors can be tinted with white or shaded with black. If you prefer a softer look, consider a pastel primary palette of light blue, pink, and pale yellow or a romantic secondary scheme of peach, lilac, and sage green.

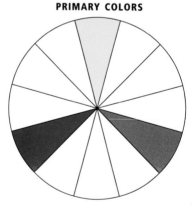

PRIMARY COLORS

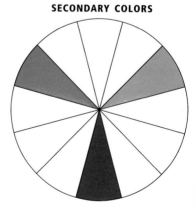

SECONDARY COLORS

Take our color quiz. Once you learn about the colors you associate with everyday activities, you can decorate with the hues that make you happy.

COLOR AND ACTIVITY INVENTORY

For insight into your color preferences, think about the color you associate with the activities listed here. *Ask yourself what color you would like to wear or be surrounded by as you go through these choices:*

Activity	Color Choice
1. Going to bed	_____
2. Eating breakfast	_____
3. Lounging in your bathrobe	_____
4. Soaking in the tub	_____
5. Applying makeup	_____
6. Polishing your nails	_____
7. Driving in your car	_____
8. Picking field flowers	_____
9. Harvesting your garden	_____
10. Coloring your hair	_____
11. Tying a scarf or tie	_____
12. Setting the table	_____
13. Going to a fancy ball	_____
14. Eating at your favorite restaurant	_____
15. Lighting candles for a romantic dinner	_____
16. Putting up a patio umbrella	_____
17. Placing a wreath on the front door	_____
18. Sitting with a refreshing drink	_____
19. Reading in front of the fire	_____
20. Mowing the lawn	_____
21. Dressing for work	_____
22. Biking with friends	_____
23. Swimming in the ocean	_____
24. Jogging after work	_____
25. Kayaking down a river	_____
26. Daydreaming at home	_____
27. Cooking for the holidays	_____
28. Talking on the telephone with your best friend	_____
29. Dining with good friends	_____
30. Celebrating getting the job	_____
31. Holding a wine tasting	_____
32. Attending a country wedding	_____
33. Arranging a bowl of fruit	_____
34. Critiquing a favorite painting	_____

SCORING

Designate each of your color choices according to three categories of color association—warm, cool, and neutral colors. First, find your colors in the following category lists:

Warm Colors: Red, Orange, Yellow, Pink

Cool Colors: Blue, Green, Purple

Neutral Colors: Black, Brown, White, Gray, Beige, Taupe

Assign an "A" wherever you have listed a *warm* color, a "B" for all your *cool* color choices, and a "C" for *neutral* colors; count how many you listed in each category.

Your Tally: Warm _____ Cool _____ Neutral _____

Warm Colors: These active colors move forward, communicate vigor, cheer you up, excite passions, inspire conversation, and force emotions.

Cool Colors: These passive colors recede into the background, cool you down, calm your nerves, lift your spirits, promote meditation, and comfort the soul.

Neutral Colors: These "open-minded" colors are easy on the eye, symbolize a down-to-earth attitude, make you feel safe and secure, and lend a cooperative air.

HOW DO YOU COMPARE?

• **Mostly "As"?** You come alive with energizing colors. Use these in the active rooms of your home: entryways, hallways, dining rooms, rooms for entertaining, and playrooms. If you happen to be living with lots of neutrals yet score high in the "A" category, don't fret; simply warm your neutral spaces with some warm-colored accessories, such as pillows or a rug.

• **Mostly "Bs"?** You respond to soothing colors. Use them in rooms for rest and relaxation, such as the bedroom, living room, home office, spa, or sunporch. For starters, consider plain white walls in a soft blue or green if you score high in this category.

• **Mostly "Cs"?** You like to play it safe. Neutral colors are perfect for rooms that connect to other rooms or spaces, such as kitchens, in which you spend a lot of time.

• **Tie with two or three categories?** Distribute cool and warm colors throughout your home in doses compatible with each room's use. You may prefer energizing warm hues in a breakfast room and calming blues and greens in a bedroom. Use neutrals to bridge warm and cool colors.

Does your eye tend to go for the bold, decoratively speaking? Consider a scheme that includes one or more of the classic crayon primaries—red, yellow, and blue. A mix of all three primaries in the same intensity creates cheerful, family-friendly rooms. Remove the yellow, and you have a classic red, white, and blue palette that's perfect for those who love nautical or Americana themes. To soften a bold primary scheme, add a mellow wood furniture piece or two, leafy plants, or a patterned fabric, such as this tablecloth, *opposite*, that includes a dash of green.

PRIMARY

Play with primaries. Playing with peppy red, blue, and yellow accessories lets you wake up a neutral room or experiment with a primary palette before committing to more permanent upholstery, paint, or wallpaper. One or two touches, such as the table linens and chair pads here, can pack a big decorative punch. Catalogs and home stores offer bright, moderately priced pillows, prints, and posters. Flea markets and craft shows yield affordable pieces, including bold 1950s tablecloths and ceramics. Fresh flowers also add a touch of bright red or yellow. For drama, mass blooms of a single color.

Yellow and Red. Often associated with kids' rooms, this vivid color scheme creates elegant adult spaces when traditional furnishings and lots of white come into play. White paint and checked slipcovers, *opposite*, update antique walnut chairs. Miniskirts show off the chairs' carved legs. Touches of green in plants and botanical artwork soften the setting.

Red, White, and Blue. Sleek with traditional overtones, this bedroom, *above*, exemplifies the versatility of classic red, white, and blue. Today the crisp quilt fosters airy, summertime ambience, but the scheme leaves room for change: Replace the quilt with a red-and-blue plaid comforter for cozy fall flavor or with a bright floral coverlet for springtime romance.

PRIMARY

Yellow and Blue.
Curtains and pillows
offer a quick and
affordable way to put a
little color into a neutral
room. This sitting spot
gets its fresh look from
blue and white toile
curtains that frame the
neutral sofa. Softly
radiant, the pale yellow
painted walls and
coordinating pillows
warm the setting
with sunny ambience,
rain or shine.

Blue and White. Put your favorite primaries to work to establish any mood from serene to sassy, and to create decorative sleight-of-hand. Calming blue paint, *above*, slows the pace for serene formal dining. Relying on the principle that cool colors recede while warm ones advance, the owners painted the adjacent hallway yellow for visual connection to the dining room.

■ Pick your favorite hue, then jump across the color wheel *(page 8)* to find a perfect mate for it. Known as complementary colors, such opposing hues produce dynamic schemes in which warm and cool hues play off against each other.

■ Decorate with one of the true complementary duos—red and green, blue and orange, or yellow and purple.

■ Or vary the formula. Love blue? If you don't like its true opposite, orange, choose its near-opposite, yellow. Have a thing for peach (pastel-orange)? Mix it with its true complement, pastel blue, or consider a mossy pastel green.

■ For harmony, pair hues of the same intensity. The blue and yellow at left are equally bold.

Blue and Yellow. If you love blue yet crave a spicy jolt, too, bring in some bright yellow. Because warm colors advance, these yellow chairs and tabletop accessories step out to offer a warm greeting. Small doses of the sunny hue also can perk up an entry or turn up the heat on a hearthside den. And golden or lemony yellows—good for home offices and kitchens—unleash creative juices.

Just as the three primary colors naturally go together, so do the three

secondary colors—green (made by combining blue and yellow), orange (made by

combining yellow and red), and purple (made by combining red and blue). Think

of such color categories not as dictators but as inspiration if you're struggling to

find just the right color mate for your favorite hue. As you plan, look beyond the

clearest secondary colors to tints and shades. For instance, if you love lilac (which

is pastel purple) but don't know what color to use with it, consider its two

SECONDARY

secondary color cousins, peach (which is pastel orange) and light green.

For the easiest color scheming, forget mixing and go with one color you love.

To keep such a monochromatic scheme lively, use various tints and shades of your

chosen hue and include a mix of textures and materials. In this room, several

greens, ranging from light to dark and from yellow-greens to bluish greens, bring

the outdoors in by repeating the subtle color variations that one finds on a walk

in the woods. A rich mix of textures and materials—smooth ceramics, satiny

woods, shiny brass and gilt, nubby baskets, and rush seats—enriches the room.

SECONDARY

Orange and Green. Fabrics in fresh tropical hues turn the once cool bay, *below*, into an especially warm time-out spot. At the windows, casual easy-sew curtains—fixed side panels plus cafe curtains for privacy—set a soft yet casual mood. The scheme shows how beautifully secondary orange and green can work with primary yellow to create a tangy, citrus-inspired palette. A glass-top table and wicker chairs—import-store finds—pull up to the bay window for dining with a garden view.

COLOR CUES

■ To enjoy your favorite colors, think of the flow from room to room throughout your home. Colors should blend but not necessarily repeat.

■ Use color to direct your eye. A cluster of colorful seating pieces can form a welcoming oasis in the middle of a large room; a coat of contrasting paint can draw attention to an architectural feature, such as a bookcase.

■ Before deciding on wall color, buy a quart of the wall paint you think you want and roll it on the wall or on a large piece of white paper to see how the color looks during the day and night.

■ Remember that the colors in light-reflecting semigloss and gloss paints often will appear lighter than those in flat paint.

Orange. One bold color may be too strong for an entire room, but it's perfect for warming up a potentially cool entryway, *opposite*. Inspired by the owners' favorite country accessories and pastoral paintings, this rich shade of coral emits a warm glow all day long—and also proves that yesterday's wood paneling can suit today's tastes when wearing a new coat of paint. (To paint paneling, sand to remove the gloss, seal with primer, then paint one or two top coats.) Bright and bold during the day, the color becomes more mellow at night when candles are lit and lamps are turned on.

SECONDARY

Green. Here's a quick color scheming trick: Roll your favorite color over your walls, then accent that hue with one or more colors that lie next to it on the color wheel *(page 8)*. Blue, which is next to green on the wheel, fills the bill in this garden-fresh kitchen. Accents of yellow and red inspired by the valance fabric warm the cool blue-green scheme, and white woodwork and cabinets keep the saturated green from overpowering the space.

Color trends come and go, but classic combinations, like classic-style clothing, are always in fashion. Whether you lean to the contemporary or the traditional, you'll find time-honored color schemes that work with your own look. Ever-crisp blue and white and always-stylish black and white are natural choices for interiors from the most contemporary architectural rooms to the most traditional bedrooms or sunporches. Add bright accents of red or yellow, and you'll have lively schemes that adapt to a variety of styles and decorating moods.

CLASSICS

When your goal is to warm up a room, turn to the appealing soft yellows, heated up by vibrant reds. Or, when drama is your goal, consider the enduring power of red or the sophistication of jewel tones to create rooms with instant presence.

Blue and white remains one of the most beloved color combinations because it is inherently fresh yet easy on the eyes. Blue and white also is flexible, stylewise, suiting traditional or country designs as easily as contemporary ones. Patterned fabrics, *opposite,* set the classic color scheme as well as the cottage mood. The pattern-blending trick? Vary the motifs' scale, from small to medium to large.

CLASSIC COMBINATIONS

Blue and White. Simple and economical, a coat of sky blue paint freshens an all-white kitchen, *opposite*. Keeping cabinets and backsplashes white brightens and balances the blue, and glowing touches of yellow in towels and golden picture frames add warm color contrast. Inspired by the walls, a few yards of blue and white fabric soften windows and stool seats.

Blue and White. Be bold with blue and use a dark background wallpaper to dramatically decorate a master bath, *above*. Note the pleasing effect of matching the wallpaper to the window treatment fabric and stenciling the white cabinets in a complementary motif. Blue willow-pattern plates, on stands, are always right for this classic motif and color combination.

Black and White. Black and white fabrics, including sheets, ticking, and vintage chenille, unify a mix of antiques while also setting a crisp, upbeat mood. Mellow wood tones on the floor and in key furniture pieces enrich and soften the usually high-key scheme. Plain painted walls provide the visual relief that keeps the black and white patterns from overpowering the space.

CLASSIC COMBINATIONS

BLACK AND WHITE

■ Always flexible, black and white can be chic or sassy, traditional or modern, depending on the style of furnishings and fabric patterns. Black and white stripes, checks, or plaids create one look, black and white toiles and tweeds another.

■ Because of their high-contrast nature, a mix of black and white fabrics and accessories needs to be tamed with some patternfree surfaces. Consider plain painted walls, a floor of golden pine or woven sisal, and plain shutters, shades, or blinds for relief.

■ Wake up a dull room of white walls and beige carpet with a dash of "pepper"—perhaps a black and white area rug and a grouping of enlarged black and white family photos.

Black, White, and Brown. Any one color can work beautifully with black and white. Shades of brown, *above,* concentrated in the plaid sofa fabric and echoed in the wood-grained floor and pine tables, foster a dashing menswear look. With contemporary style as a goal, the designer worked in lots of crisp white, from painted walls and alternating checkerboards on the floor and black and white stripes on the wing chair to stunning black and white photos hung as art. Black metal lamps carry out the modern scheme.

Black, White, and Red. Modern with traditional overtones, this living room, *opposite,* gets its snappy style from the strong contrast of red, white, and black on the graphic buffalo check fabrics. Because a bold black and white scheme has visual weight, for balance and impact consider massing one accent color instead of dotting it around the room. Here, the bright red is concentrated on the drop-arm camelback settee.

Neutrals are among the most relaxing color schemes. By common decorating definition, neutral schemes tend to be in the natural shades of off-whites, creams, beiges, and pale taupes. How do you get the soothing quality of a neutral, monochromatic scheme and avoid boredom? Use shapes, textures, and patterns for warmth and interest. The easy plan? Start with neutral walls and major furniture as your first decorating step. Look for lamp bases in different yet harmonious materials, such as natural wood and pottery. Use the same approach

NEUTRALS

with window treatments, table skirts, throws, or accent pillows. Vary the shapes, sizes, fabrics, and trims on accent pillows. Glass, crystal, distressed tin, pottery, wood, wicker, and even concrete garden ornaments introduce texture without adding busy color and pattern. Add interest with weathered architectural fragments, such as windows or gates, or with subdued prints or etchings rather than bright paintings. Mix the smooth with the rough, the rustic and the refined. The textures of shiny glass, satiny wood, and a cut-pile rug add interest and maintain the calm created by this room's beige walls, carpet, and seating pieces.

NEUTRALS

Taupe and Cream. Neutral yet lively, this bedroom sitting spot gets its crisp look from the large-scale plaid fabric that covers both the daybed and the wall behind it. The textures of glossy woodwork, matte walls, nubby carpet, and slick metal delight the eye without overpowering the neutral scheme.

NEUTRALS

Dynamic Neutrals. The degree of contrast between light and dark affects the mood of any neutral scheme. A rich array of neutrals, *left,* from pale off-white upholstery to dark stained woods, creates an especially lively version of a no-color palette.

Sophisticated Monochromatics. For serene sophistication, avoid sharp contrasts between light and dark. In this window seat, *below,* serene off-whites create calm, while the subtle textures of the pillows' decorative trims and the window shades' lush gathers add visual interest.

Earthy Neutrals. Cooled by a dash of blue and green, grainy woods and rugged ceramics create a casual look in this kitchen, *opposite*

NEUTRAL FABRIC TIPS

■ For a livelier version of a neutral scheme, mix patterns, such as stripes, toiles, checks, and leafy designs.

■ For a softer look, consider limiting fabrics to a blend of woven fabrics, such as damask, chenille, and velvet, that offer eye-pleasing textures without strong patterns. You also can punch up a monochromatic scheme by mixing lighter tints and darker shades of beige or taupe.

■ Use a neutral color scheme to refresh and unify a mixed collection of traditional-style furniture pieces. A restricted palette and limited pattern not only create a relaxed yet sophisticated look but also allow the classic shapes or details of fine furnishings to be seen.

Jewel tones are perfect for a jolt of unexpected color. Deep saturated colors soak in the light, making a large room instantly cozier or a room with a cool exposure instantly richer. Jewel tones—ruby reds, deep emerald greens, sapphire blues, amethyst purples—create drama for living and dining rooms. Lit by chandeliers, soft lamp light, the glow of candles, the sparkle of a mirror, or a touch of shiny metal, these colors shimmer in contrast to the night outside. In today's decorating, these deep hues are used to cozy up smaller rooms, such as

JEWEL TONES

bedrooms or sitting rooms. Also use jewel accents for neutral interiors or as warmth-creating seasonal changes. Pick out pillows and a throw in one or more of your favored hues. Add glass accessories or lampshades for chic, deep-toned touches. Think of the royal robes of purple and blue, studded crowns of precious stones, deep hues that shimmer and shine. For the richest jewel-tone walls— those with shimmering depth of color—roll on three or more coats of paint. This appealing bathroom gets its richness from amethyst painted walls that surround the sink area. A squeeze of citrus color adds warmth.

Ruby Red. A warm-hued painting, *opposite* inspired a fresh wall color of deep, rich eggplant, creating an intimate setting that's especially dramatic for nighttime dinner parties. The golden tones of the oversize art echo in the honeyed patina of an antique sideboard. **Amethyst Purple.** Inherently soothing, analogous periwinkle blue, green, and purple create an especially restful bedroom scheme, *below*. Flowers and linens add warm contrast.

COOL OR WARM?

■ Use large doses of warm garnet or ruby red in active, vibrant rooms such as a nighttime dining room or a kitchen for family gatherings.

■ Cozy up a study or a library with a dark shade of any jewel-tone color. (A shade is a color to which black has been added.)

■ Use a cool emerald, amethyst, or sapphire when the goal is serenity. For lightness, use an airy pastel tint of a jewel tone and include solid white furnishings and surfaces.

■ Keep color-mixing basics in mind when working with jewel tones. For a mellow mood, create an analogous scheme of colors, such as blue, green, and purple, that lie next to each other on the color wheel. For a livelier look in which warm and cool colors collide, pick colors, such as purple and yellow, which lie across the color wheel from each other.

JEWEL TONES

Sapphire. Create a cozy retreat in a room with high ceilings and tall windows by darkening the walls, *left*. Blues of this hue give instant intensity without overpowering. Repeat the shade as the fabric background for a harmony. When walls are in good condition, use satin or semigloss paint for nighttime shine and depth. If walls are not in perfect condition, opt for flat paint, not gloss.

Cinnabar. Old-world stucco walls of this new cottage-style dining room prove that red isn't just for formal spaces, *lower left*. The vivid backdrop dramatically silhouettes the hutch, which is painted the same white as the wainscoting for crisp contrast.

Emerald. The shimmering green wall covering sets a restful mood in a master or guest bedroom, *opposite*. The deep background showcases framed botanical prints. Repeat such strong color in an accent. Here, the lampshade is the same intensity of green as decorative wall finish.

Inspired to put a little fresh color into your life?

Here's how to start the affordable way—with a can of paint.

QUICK TIPS ON PAINT

Find the right color. With today's technology, paint stores can mix and tint paints to match any shade you love. Let a favorite fabric or rug inspire your choice. To decide on the exact shade you want, gather three to five samples of paint chips in your color range. Tape the chips on the wall and observe the colors at different times of the day and under artificial light at night. When you've narrowed your choices to two or three shades, buy a small can of each and paint a wallboard scrap or wall section with each. It's easy for even an experienced decorator to be fooled by the effects of light, floor coverings, and furnishings on paint colors, so, unless you are absolutely certain of your choice, do not skip this step. If you are considering a strong hue, remember that it will appear even more intense once it's rolled onto all four walls. Often the best advice in such cases is to switch to the next-lightest paint chip on the same paint card.

Choose a finish. The finish of the paint will affect its light-reflecting qualities and the ultimate color of the painted surface. What finish you choose is a matter of personal preference, but keep these guidelines in mind: Flat paint generally is preferred for less-than-perfect walls. Paint with some sheen, such as satin or even shinier semigloss, is scrubbable and ideal for kitchens, baths, or children's rooms. Also consider the shimmer of semigloss paint for a dramatic dining room used at night, a powder room, and to highlight woodwork.

Calculate the amount of paint. Paint cans usually state the one-coat coverage you can expect from a gallon. For many paints, including primers, a gallon will cover about 400 square feet. But it's still a good idea to calculate coverage yourself. Measure the perimeter of the room (all walls). Multiply the result by the ceiling height to get the square footage. Round off to the full foot. (Don't deduct for windows or other openings, unless they add up to more than 100 square feet.) Divide that figure into the number of square feet that a gallon of paint promises to cover. Round up to the nearest whole number. Buy accurately, as it is difficult to match paint if you need more or to dispose of properly if you buy too much. Also remember that if you are painting a wall an intense color, such as cranberry red, you will need more coats than the paint can promises in order to create the desired depth of color. Finally, it's always a good idea to save paint for touch-ups, especially if you think you may rearrange artwork or rehang window hardware.

Gather supplies. Here's what you will need for a basic paint job:
• *Primer*
• *Brown paper drop cloths for the floor; heavy plastic drop cloths for furniture*
• *Surfacing compound and a knife to apply it, sandpaper, painter's tape, edger*
• *Metal paint can, plastic liners, roller with threaded handle for extensions, sash and trim brushes*

Prepare the walls. A smooth, clean, dry, mildew-free wall does count. The prettiest paint color won't compensate for a wall that is not in good condition. Before you paint, scrape or sand away rough spots. Strip old wallpaper, if necessary. (Depending on the paper type, its age, and how it was applied, you may find a spray-on liquid combined with scoring to be less cumbersome than a rented steamer. If you do rent a steamer, follow the directions to avoid accidents.) If any glossy surfaces remain, dull them with sandpaper or liquid sandpaper. Scrub walls with mild detergent and water. Rinse with a sponge and clear water. Remove mold and mildew with a solution of one quart of household bleach and three quarts of water. For a smooth finish, use a primer, and treat stains with a special primer to prevent bleed-through. Never paint over damp or wet walls.